Wolfgang Paul Constance

The best method for success
on the stock market

AF216662

Publishing house:
Books on Demand
Norderstedt, Germany
ISBN 9783749465835
© 2019 Wolfgang Paul Constance
Cover picture:
Sculpture in front of the Frankfurt
Stock Exchange
Sculptor: Reinhard Dachlauer
Photo: Wolfgang Paul Constance

Table of contents

The best speculators

Dear Sofia,

in your letter you asked me what arguments speak for the stock market. First I write what speaks against them:

The stock market has a female article in most languages and is a capricious, completely unpredictable lady. Sometimes she has a good mood, in the stock market language 'bull market'. Sometimes she is very distressed, in the stock market language 'bearish market'. She is heavily influenced by political events, even if they happen on the other side of the globe. She is always curious about positive and negative rumours, to which she responds with rising and falling prices.

If you want to do business with this capricious lady you have an advantage as a woman: Statistics prove that women on the stock market are on average more successful than men, as they prefer safe investment strategies, but men risk speculation.

Instead of boring you with a treatise on the way to succeed on the stock market, I prefer to tell you the success story of the two best speculators:

Benjamin Graham began at the age of 20 his career on *Wall Street*. For 12 dollars a week he wrote stock prices on a black board. At the age of 25, he already had yearly income of 600 000 dollars. In 1934, he explained his *value investing strategy* in his bestseller *Security Analysis*. Taking this strategy into account, in 1948 he invested a quarter of his assets in the insurance company *Geico*. Over the next 8 years, he made a 1635% profit from this investment. For 30 years, his strategy has yielded an average annual profit of 17%. 10 000 dollars became 1 110 000 dollars. From 1928 to 1957 he taught at *Columbia University*.There was only one student to whom he gave the best grade A+: **Warren Buffett**. He bought the first three shares at the age of 11. From 1945 he speculated in the investment company of his teacher *Benjamin Graham*. When he finished, *Warren Buffett* raised 105 000 dollars from his relatives and started his own investment firm. This achieved an average annual return of 29,5 % from 1956-1969. The relatives of *Warren Buffett* became multimillionaires. In 1998, everyone who had invested 10 000 dollars in 1956 had the fantastic sum of 150 million dollars. *Warren Buffett* has acquired 86 billion in asset speculation. The share of its *Berkshire Hathaway* investment company currently costs 300 000 dollars and is the most expensive share of the world.

Unlike other famous speculators *Warren Buffett* makes no secret of his stock purchases. They are published and commented by him. This made him a guru for millions of small investors in America. These repeat his share purchases, which increases their price.

Warren Buffett is one of the richest men in the world. Nevertheless, he still lives in the same house in *Omaha*, which he acquired in 1958 for 31 000 dollars. He rides a mid-range car and treats himself to a good meal at the steakhouse once a week.

In an interview with US magazine *Fortune*, on June 25, 2006, he announced that he would donate 85 % of his fortune to charitable organisations and medical research, 30 billion dollars of which to the *Bill Gates' foundation*.

Why did I tell you these success stories? They illustrate better than a stock market seminar: The most effective method of stock market speculation is to pursue with patience a good investment strategy. In another letter I will give you more information about the *value investing strategy*.

To make you aware that you are in the best company as a speculator, I will introduce you to some prominent speculators:

The roman philosopher *Cicero* acquired by the real estate speculation a considerable fortune. He came to two findings that have kept their validity until today: money is the basis of the republic and speculation is the springboard to a great fortune.

The French writer *Voltaire*, a passionate speculator, had all the lots of the French state lottery bought up by straw men. He had calculated that the sum of the lottery winnings was considerably larger than the total price for the purchase of all lots. He was very rich by this coup, but the lottery director was dismissed without notice.

Other famous speculators: the painter *Gauguin*, the writers *Balzac* and *Beaumarchais* and the English economist

Lord Keynes. Below his portrait, the British Government wrote the following text:

John Maynard Lord Keynes, who managed to make a fortune without to work.

Since I am doing a tour of *California*, you cannot reach me in the next four weeks.

The so-called Black Friday

Dear Wolfgang,

during your *California* trip, I read a book about the biggest stock market crash. It became clear to me: The stock market has two faces: a friendly one that has shown her to *Benjamin Graham* and *Warren Buffett* and an unfriendly one that has shown her to many stockbrokers. One of them wrote:

'On the stock market you can make a small fortune by investing a great fortune.'

The stock market has repeatedly destroyed gigantic sums of money. In 1929, *Wall Street* caused the worst financial debacle in history. Before 1929, the world experienced the biggest stock market boom of all time. The speculative fever has infected all social layers. Hot share tips were even more in demand than the alcohol prohibited by the *Prohibition*. The chauffeurs only listened with one ear to the traffic; with the other they tried to catch a stock market tip of their passengers. The valet of a speculator won a quarter of a million dollars with the tip of his master. The stock market tip of a grateful patient brought 30 000 dollars to a nurse.

An actress adorned her apartment with graphs of rising share prices: *General Electric* rose 300 % in one year and *Radio Corporation* 400 %.

God's own country was struck by the delusion that the abolition of poverty is imminent and then a new era of 'eternal prosperity' begins.

On October 24, 1929, the so-called **Black Friday**, began the largest financial debacle in history. The whole drama is illustrated by the course of the *Dow-Jones Index*: At the first listing in 1896, the index has 41 points. Until 1927 he rises to 100 points. Through an overheated, partly bank financed stock market speculation, the index reached in September 1929 the record high of 381 points. The share prices are far above the real value of the companies.

Irving Fisher, a professor at *Yale University*, said on October 16:

"It looks like the shares have reached a permanent high plateau."

In the next three days there will be a crash of the stock market.

The *Dow-Jones-Index* loses 15 %. On October 23, the index drops to 300 points. The following day, the *Black Friday*, the total value of all companies listed on *Wall Street* falls by 11 billion dollars. On Monday the index drops to 260 points. On Tuesday he lost another 12 %. On 15 November he drops to 180 points. In the summer of 1932, after a total loss of 89%, he finally falls on the 41 points he had of the first day of his listing.

The share prices of the big American companies plunge into the abyss: *Radio Corporation* from 115 to 3 1/2, *General Electric* from 220 to 20.

In American statistics, the stock market crash is reflected as follows:

More than 123 000 successful speculators holding a luxury car had to transfer to the subway. As a result of the financial debacle, more than 9000 banks declared bankruptcy. The American legend of rag, who rises to the millionaire, played out more and more often in the opposite direction. Millions of shareholders in America and Europe were destitute, but struggled to find rich people to beg for.

The rising number of suicides inspired

American comedian *Will Rogers* to the following gag:

'In New York, the hotel porter asks new arrivals:
Do you want a room to sleep or jump out of the window?'

I care a lot about sleeping well. Therefore, I cannot decide to join the club of shareholders, which consists mainly of risk-taking men.

The investor's safety net

Dear Sofia,

upon my return from *California*, I found your letter, which I answer immediately. The crash of the *Dow-Jones-Index* between 1929 and 1932 to the value of 1896 shook your confidence in the stock market. I can understand that well. However, the further development of the *Dow-Jones-Index* is a success story: In 1954 he reached the level of 1929 again. In 1972 he broke through the sound barrier of 1000 points.In 1987 he climbs over 2000 points. In 1992 he clears the hurdle of 3000 points. Thereafter, he rises to more than 26 500 points by 2019. Although the price increase was repeatedly interrupted by stock market crashes, the *Dow-Jones-Index* raised a lot from 1896 to 2019.

Stock market boom and stock market crash are two sides of the same coin. The stockbroker *André Kostolany* writes:

'No stock market crash that was not preceded by a boom and no boom that does not end with a stock market crash.'

A speculator said:

"There is no ringing before the crash."
However, there is an alarm signal before the stock market crash: the so-called *Housewife's stock market*. This means that people are entering the stock market speculation, which have no idea about stocks. The American billionaire *John Rockefeller* obviously had a keen sense for this warning sign. He sold all the shares a few weeks ago *Black Friday*, as a bootblack had given him several share tips.

Due to the experience of the *Black Friday*, the stock exchanges set a new rule to prevent an avalanche-like sell off. In extreme price losses, trading is suspended on the stock market. Thanks to this strategy, none of the later stock market crashes had more the devastating consequences than the *Black Friday*.

After the stock market crash of 1987, the Frankfurt stockbrokers proved that they had not lost their humour. They wrote the following text:

My finances are shattered.
It crashed on the stock market.
I got that from my shares
made kites to children.
I went with them to field,

where the breezes blow gently.
There I was able to see my shares
go up again.

Perhaps I can give you back the lost confidence in the stock market by introducing you the DAX yield triangle. This triangle shows the average annual returns that a security deposit replicated to the DAX would have earned if it had been bought and sold between 1983 and 2006. The triangle consists of 300 fields. The blue fields mean wins, the red fields mean loss. 87 % of the fields are profit fields. Only 10 % of the fields are loss fields. I hope the small number of loss fields will give you again confidence in the stock market.

One can compare the stock speculator with a tightrope walker. If he falls, his life is saved by the safety net. If the investor was smart enough to build a safety net, his fortune will be largely salvaged in the event of a stock market crash.

This safety net consists of the following 7 golden rules:

1. Invest only part of your assets in shares. The share of the securities portfolio is calculated according to the following formula:

Share in % = 100 minus age.

2. Buy stocks only with money you do not need over a long period of time.

3. Invest your money in different shares from different industries.

4. Invest your stock gains into fixed income securities. When the returns are reinvested in stocks, and when there is a stock market crash thereafter, most of the gains are lost.

5. Realize the equity gains. One should always remember: The stock market is not a one-way street. Gains are only borrowed money that you have to repay at the next price loss.

6. Never buy shares with the help of bank loans.

7. Minimize your losses by selling the shares as soon as possible in the event of a price loss. A proven exchange rule is:

Let price gains run, keeping price losses small. To compensate for a loss of 50 %, a price increase of 100 % is required.

Finally, I tell you an anecdote about the Berlin banker *Carl Fürstenberg*:

He had received a compartment in the first class of the sleeping car due to highest protection for the journey from Warsaw to Berlin. As the train left, Mr L.

approached him, whom the banker had just met at a business dinner at the hotel *Adlon*.

"Mister Fürstenberg, I just see that your second bed is vacant. I'll pay you any price if you leave it to me."

At that moment, Fürstenberg remembered that Mr L. had eaten noisily, which caused him to associate an even loader snore. Thoughtfully, he looked at Mr L. and said:

"I'll think about your proposal."

When the train stopped at the border station the next morning, he woke up with the squealing of the braking wheels. He heard the cutting voice of the customs officer:

"Border station, passport control."

Tired and pale, Mr L. sat on his suitcase. *Fürstenberg* said:

"If I see you like this, I'm sorry afterwards that I did not offer you my second bed."

Mr L. answered:

"The night was not so bad; but the worst part is that the customs officer reproached me because yesterday I forgot to pick up my passport at the hotel reception. I could not get this stubborn official by my requests nor by a dizzy high bribe to let me enter Germany."

At that moment, the stubborn official left a neighboring compartment. The banker went to him and said a few words. Then the official came to Mr L. and tapped his service cap:

"You can enter Germany."

Mr L. would like to have the banker around his neck. He went to him and squeezed his hand with great gratitude.

"Thank you very much, Mister Fürstenberg, but what did you say to this stubborn Prussian official?"

"I gave him an official order and he said:

Of course, if you give me an official order."

Basic knowledge of the stock market

Dear Sofia,

I am glad that you want to enter the stock market speculation because of my letter. You write:
'I have no idea about stocks.'
According to a survey, half of all Germans regarding equities are unsuspecting. Therefore, the share of shareholders in Germany in 2016 was only 6 % (France 15 %, Switzerland 20 %, Great Britain 23 % and USA 25 %).
Germans have a savings of 6000 billion Euros. But only 6 % of them have shares. However, the shares earn more profit in the long run than any other investment. The average return on equities over the past 50 years has been 2 % above the average rate of return on fixed income securities. In a short investment period, this interest difference has little effect on profit. In the long term, however, the yield gap due to compound interest is very large. The final amount of a 9 % return investment exceeds the final amount of a 7 % return investment by 40 % in 10 years, by 173 % in 20 years

and by 565 % in 30 years.

The stock market is an important engine of the economy. The financiers (shareholders) and the money recipients (entrepreneurs) meet here. The entrepreneurs increase their capital by transforming their company into a stock corporation. Shareholders can benefit from company profit distributions and rising share prices.

By purchasing a share, the investor becomes the coowner of the company. He is involved in the profit, if the development of the enterprise is good and at the loss, if the development is bad.

A *stock index* is made up of a larger number of shares. The 100 largest English stock corporations form the FTSE 100, the 30 largest American companies the *Dow-Jones-Index* and the 30 largest German stock corporations the German Stock Index (abbreviation DAX).

An *index certificate* is a participation in all shares of an index. The DAX certificate is therefore a participation in all 30 shares of the DAX Index. The price of the DAX certificate is calculated from the prices of the 30 DAX shares. A big advantage of an index certificate is the reduction of the price risk by the participation in a large number of shares.

The disadvantage of index certificates: If the bank issuing the index certificate goes bankrupt, the index certificates fall under the bankruptcy estate threatening the investor with significant losses.

ETF (Exchange Traded Fund) is a fund that reflects the performance of a stock market index. Example: An ETF based on the DAX reflects as closely as possible the price of that index.

The ETF offer the opportunity to invest in all the stocks of an index by buying only one security.

The ETFs are traded on the stock market and can therefore be bought or sold at any time.

Due to its passive management, the costs are much lower than in the case of an actively managed fund.

The following example illustrates the great impact of annual administration costs: Without annual administration costs, fund shares amounting to € 10 000 and yielding 6 % in 30 years will increase to € 100 626. With an annual administration fee of 2,5 %, the investor only has € 49 839 after 30 years.

The dividends are either distributed to the fund owners or reinvested in the fund.

The ETFs are treated as special assets. In the event of insolvency of the issuer, they remain the property of the investor.

When buying an ETF, you either give the order to buy the cheapest price or you name the price you want to pay the maximum. When selling you either give the order to sell at the highest price or you name the price you want to receive at least.

When building an ETF package, there are two options. You can buy an equal number of ETFs every month, or you can spend an equal amount of money every month to buy ETFs. I recommend you the second option. If you spend an equal amount on ETFs each month, fewer ETFs are bought each month in the case of rising prices, but more ETFs in the case of falling prices. As a result, a cheaper purchase prise than the acquisition of an equal number of ETFs per month.

The portion of the profit that a company distributes to its shareholders is called *dividend*. The calculation of the dividend yield is very simple:

Dividend yield in % = dividend divided by share price x 100.

The dividend will be distributed the day after the General Meeting. Any shareholder who has a share in his depository on the day of the General Meeting will receive the dividend. The day after the dividend payment, the share price will decrease by an amount equal to the dividend.

I will now explain to you the most important causal factors for the development of share prices:

The relationship between supply and demand determines the share price. Increasing demand has a positive effect on the share price; falling demand has a negative effect. Here, the economic situation plays an important role:

In the economic upturn and boom investors can buy more shares because of their rising income. Share prices rise. In periods of economic downturn and recession, investors can spend less money on shares. Share prices are falling.

An important causative factor in rising prices is a falling oil price. Since investors have to spend less money on energy costs (gasoline, heating), they can buy more shares.

An important causative factor in falling prices is an increase in interest rates of fixed income securities. In this case, investors will buy more fixed income securities and therefore have less money to buy shares.

You have now learned the basics of stock market trading. Apart from this basic knowledge you only need to know the three best stock market strategies in order to make big profits on the stock market. I will introduce you these strategies in my next letter.

Finally I will tell you two anecdotes about *Carl Fürstenberg*:

Mr. A., a new richman with an inversely proportional ratio of wealth and intelligence, regularly asked Fürstenberg for stock market advice.Surprisingly enough however, he always did the opposite of what the banker advised him to do. Therefore he had little success on the stock market and even less reputation. When he once again wanted a hot tip, Fürstenberg said griffly:

"Kiss my navel."

"I do not understand that."

"You need to understand that very well,

you always do the opposite of what I say."

Mr. G., a member of the Berlin Stock Exchange, received the title of 'Consul General' from a completely insignificant state. He was keen to always be addressed with this title. At a reception in Fürstenberg's bank there was a meeting between Mr. A., the stockbroker with the worst reputation, and Mr. G., the stockbroker with the highest title. Mr. A. raised his champagne glass and said in a venerable voice:

"I take the liberty of drinking a good swig of your health, Mr. Consul."

Fürstenberg said with an ironic smile.

"Julius Caesar was only Consul. Mr. G. is Consul General."

.

The best strategies

Dear Sofia,

at a carnival session in *Mainz* the cabaret artist *Herbert Bonnewitz* joked:

"Dear Lady, whom let you think for you?"

Regarding stock speculation, you should have no inhibitions to let the stock market professionals think for you. It is better to make a lot of money with their help than by speculating on the stock market with little success. I will introduce you to the three best stock market strategies so you know how your future stock market profits will be generated. Stock picking with the three best strategies takes a lot of time and effort. That's why you'd better leave them to the stock market specialists.

The **value investing strategy** developed by *Benjamin Graham* is based on the following consideration:

If the stock market value of a share is lower than its real value, this share is bought over the medium term as investors recognize the undervaluation. Consequently, the price of this share rises.

Due to the undervaluation, the risk of a price loss is low. The shares selected with the help of the *value investing strategy* thus have a good price opportunity and at the same time a low price risk.

The MSCI EMU VALUE index reflects the performance of undervalued European companies. This index rose 95% from 1997 to 2009. The index of companies that were not undervalued only rose 51% in the same period. The difference of 44% proves the superiority of the *value investing strategy*.

That's why I recommend you buy an ETF fund based on the *value investing strategy*, for example:

DEKA STOXX EUROPE STRONG VALUE 20 UCITS ETF-EUR DIS ISIN DE000ETFL045

Rise in market prices within the last 10 years: 130 %.

All rises in market prices were calculated on **25.5.2019** (source: www.onvista.de)

The **dividend strategy** developed by *Benjamin Graham* is based on the following consideration:

The total return of a share consists of the price gain and the dividend. Shares that pay a high dividend therefore also have an above-average total return. There are two variants of the *dividend strategy*:

The strategy top 10

At the beginning of the year, you buy the 10 stocks of an index that pay out the highest dividend. These stocks are then kept in the depository for one year.

The low 5 strategy

Of the 10 stocks with the highest dividend yield, you buy the 5 stocks with the lowest purchase price. These are held for one year in the depository.

The so-called DIVDAX is an index of the 15 DAX shares with the highest dividend distribution.

Between 2000 and 2011, the total return of the DIVDAX exceeded the total return of the DAX by 45 %. That's why I recommend you buy an ETF fund based on the *dividend strategy*, for example:

XTRACKERS STOXX GLOBAL SELECT DIVIDEND 100 SWAP UCITS ETF

ISIN LU0292096186

Rise in market prices within the last 10 years: 209%.

The principle of **momentum strategy** is to buy shares that are already on an uptrend. This upward trend can be seen from the fact that the share price has risen above average in the last six month. The strategy is based on the following consideration:

If the share price has risen above average in the past, it is very likely to rise in the near future. When the price of share has risen, it tends to go up further. This dynamics of the course is called *momentum*.

The effectiveness of the *momentum strategy* was proved by calculations of the *University of Mannheim*: with this method, yields can be achieved that are 10 % above the average return of the index.

This method confirms the saying of British stockbrokers:

'The trend is your friend.'

I recommend you to buy an ETF fund based on the *momentum strategy,* for example*:*

XTRACKERS MSCI WORLD MOMENTUM UCITS ETF – 1C USD ACC

ISIN IE00BL25JP72

Rise in market prices within **the last 3 years**: 56 %.

ETFs usually outperform funds managed

by fund managers. I only recommend actively managed funds under the following conditions:

1. You should only buy funds that are traded in Euros, as funds in foreign currencies carry a currency risk.

2. You should only buy funds with a safety net: mixed funds that do not contain only shares but also fixed-interest securities (as a safety net).

3. The fund should be traded on the stock market. If you buy an actively managed fund from an investment company, you must pay a sales charge (up to 5 %). This does not apply when buying on the stock market. Traded Funds have another advantage: The investment company may suspend the taking back of the fund if exceptional circumstances require it to be suspended. In this case you can sell the fund via the stock market.

4. At least one of the major rating agencies should certify that the fund is above average quality. The best or worst rating (in parentheses): Morningstar: 5 stars (1 star), Scope: A (E), Eurofonds: 1 (5), Feri: A (E), Lipper Leaders: 5 (1), Standard & Poors: Platinum (Grading removed).

Below I recommend you three funds that meet these 4 conditions:

KEPLER VORSORGE MIXFONDS -EUR DIS
ISIN AT0000969787
Rise in market prices within the last 10 years: 116 %.

ACATIS GANE VALUE EVENT FONDS -A EU
ISIN DE000A0X7541
Rise in market prices within the last 10 years: 128 %.

INVESCO PAN EUROPEAN HIGH INCOME FUND
ISIN LU0243957312
Rise on market prices within the last 10 years: 164 %.

At the end of the year, I advice you to return to your investment company,through your bank, those funds that have had the lowest return since their purchase. This increases the average return on the funds remaining in the depository.

I recommend that you use some of the profits generated by ETFs and funds to by high-yielding equity funds,for example:

ISHARES MDAX(DE) UCITS ETF -EUR ACC

ISIN DE0005933923

Rise in market prices within the last 10 years: 301 %.

FRANKLIN TECHNOLOGY FUND –
A EUR ACC

ISIN LU0260870158

Rise in market prices within the last 10 years: 535 %.

With regard to the return, the following must be taken into account: The price gained on the sale of a fund is tax-exempt in *Switzerland* if a speculative period is observed. In *Germany,* however, a tax is deducted from the price gain.

Finally, I tell you two anecdotes about *Carl Fürstenberg*:

The banker was a punctuality fanatic. The rumour circulated in Berlin:

'The carriage of Fürstenberg drives every morning at 9 o'clock through the Brandenburg Gate.'

This rumour reached the ears of the emperor, who lived by the motto:

'Punctuality is the courtesy of kings.'

One morning, the carriages met both at the Brandenburg Gate. The emperor greeted Fürstenberg, whom he knew from many receptions at the court, with a gracious wave. He than pulled out his pocket watch to check the punctuality of the banker. However, this had stopped. He set her at 9 o'clock. When at 12 o'clock the bell of the 'Nikolaikirche' began to beat, he pulled the watch out of his pocket. Both hands stood on the number 12.

Punctuality fanatic *Fürstenberg* was in a sweat when his carriage got stuck in a jam on the way to an author reading at the Hotel *Adlon*.

When he arrived, he saw several men talking loudly at the entrance.

"Psst, please speak softly", he said."You can see: some of the audience is already sleeping."

At the reception, which took place after the reading, a journalist asked him what impression he had of the reading by the author, who had written books about several European capitals in just a few months.

"As he writes constantly under pressure of time, he tends to generalize, for example, he writes that the women in Berlin are big and full-bosomed and wear very short skirts when he saw such a 'lady' standing at the exit of the Berlin train station."

The most common mistakes

Dear Sofia,

before you go into the stock market speculation, I have to warn you the most common mistakes that are made by the shareholders. I have already introduced you to the safety net of the 7 rules.Unfortunately, these are ignored by most shareholders. In a booming stock market, stockbrokers tend to overweight the equity holding in their depository. This happens either because they do not know the formula:

'Share in % = 100 minus age' or deliberately disregard this formula.

A common stock market trap is a 'sure-fire secret tip'. Here there is a risk that other shares are sold in order to be able to put as much capital as possible on the one card of the sure-fire tip. If the sure-fire tip proves to be a flop, it means a significant loss for investors.

Few shareholders convert their equity gains into fixed-interest securities. They fear the threat of yield reduction when switching to fixed-interest securities. They do not understand that this yield reduction is the unavoidable price for securing their stock profits.

The *counter-cyclical strategy* is to buy at falling prices and sell when prices rise. Since the shareholder follows the herd instinct, it is difficult for him to sell with rising prices. If everyone buys, why should he sell against the tide?

However, there is a behaviour that is even more difficult for him: to sell a share whose price has fallen below the purchase price. This is interpreted by the shareholder in the sense that the purchase was a mistake. No shareholder likes to admit that he made a mistake. That's why he's looking for arguments not to sell shares, for example:

'The stock market was wrong and will correct this mistake again.'

As a rule, it is not the stock market that was wrong, but the shareholder.

Another argument:

'It is a temporary price weakness, which is soon compensated by a rise in price.'

As stock prices sometimes recover on a declining share price, these price recoveries keep raising hopes for loss compensation. Accompanied by ever new hopes on a loss compensation, the share price drops to ever lower levels.

Another argument:

'As long as I do not sell the share, the price loss is not yet realized. Only when I sell the share will the loss be realized.'

If you do not sell a share that falls below your purchase price, you will be doubly damaging: Firstly, because of the loss of this share and secondly because of the lost profits you would have made if you sold the share early and invested it into a profitable share.

If a share falls 10-15 % below the buy price, I recommend that you sell the share.

In his book 'Geld, das große Abenteuer:' *André Kostolany* describes how difficult that is:

'The hardest thing is to accept a loss on the stock exchange resigning. It is a surgical procedure.You have to amputate the arm before the poisoning spreads, the sooner the better. This is difficult and among 100 people there is only one who is capable of doing so.'

You can see how difficult it is for the shareholder to sell a stock that has fallen below the purchase price. However, there is a behaviour that is even harder for him: to buy sinking shares. Few have the power to buy shares when the entire stock market crashes. Again, the herd instinct proves to be the greatest obstacle. If one hears the call "fire" and sees all shareholders rushing to the stock exchange exit, one must have the steel-hard nerves of *Warren Buffett*, in order to remain in the stock exchange and to buy the shares, which panic sell the shareholders at rock-bottom prices.

André Kostolany describes the ups and downs on the stock market as follows:

The stock market professionals ('strong hands') buy their shares in a stock market crash at rock-bottom prices. The stock market boom following the crash is increasingly attracting amateurs ('shaky hands') to the stock market. The stock market professionals sell these amateurs their shares during the stock market boom to maximum prices. The crash following the stock market boom throws the amateurs in a state of panic. They sell their shares, which they have bought at the highest prices from the professionals, back to the professionals, but this time at rock-bottom prices. After that, the game begins again, in which the amateurs always lose by paying the winnings of the professionals, who are always the profiteers.

Finally, I'll tell you an anecdote about a man who owed his biggest stock market coup to the panic of the stock market traders. He was a descendant of that legendary money dynasty which received two honorary titles: *Kings of the bankers* and *Bankers of the kings*.

Nathan Rothschild bought war bonds on the London Stock Exchange which financed England's fight against *Napoleon*. On June 18, 1815, there was a decisive battle at *Waterloo* between the troops of Napoleon and the armies of the allies *England* and *Prussia*. It is believed that the banker received the news of England's victory by a carrier pigeon of his Belgian agent.

He went straight to the London Stock Exchange and sold his war bonds with a deeply depressed countenance. Panic - stricken, stockbrokers followed his lead and sold off their war bonds, which crashed in no time. The war bonds were bought by banker's straw men at rock-bottom prices.

The news of Napoleon's defeat led to a

stock market boom on the London Stock Exchange.

Biggest winner of the day was *Nathan Rothschild*. The panic of the stock market traders had him given the fantastic profit of one million in pounds sterling.